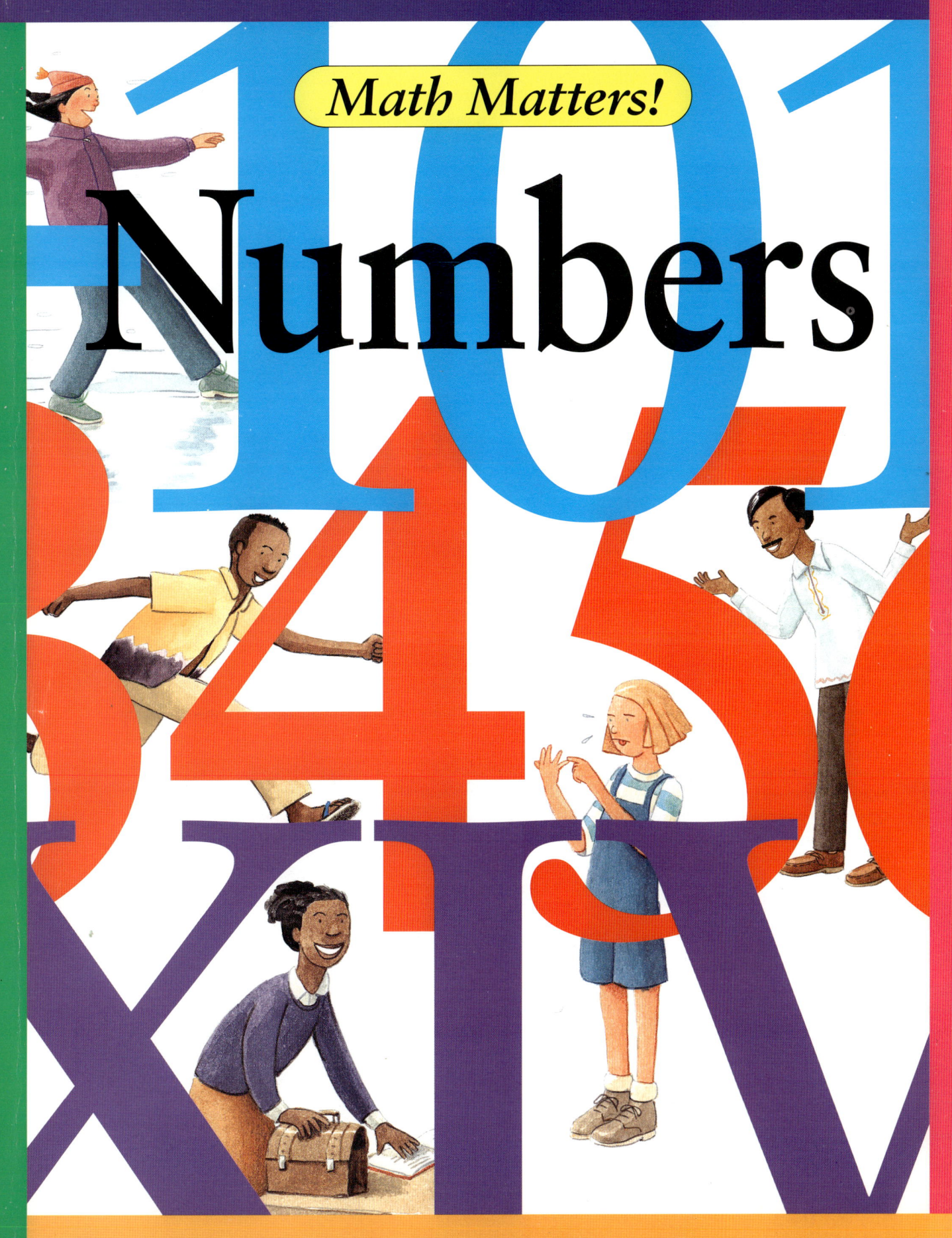

Look out for these sections to help you learn more about each topic:

Remember...
This provides a summary of the key concept(s) on each two-page entry. Use it to revise what you have learned.

Word check
These are new and important words that help you understand the ideas presented on each two-page entry.

All of the word check entries in this book are shown in the glossary on page 45. The versions in the glossary are sometimes more extensive explanations.

Book link...
Although this book can be used on its own, other titles in the *Math Matters!* set may provide more information on certain topics. This section tells you which other titles to refer to.

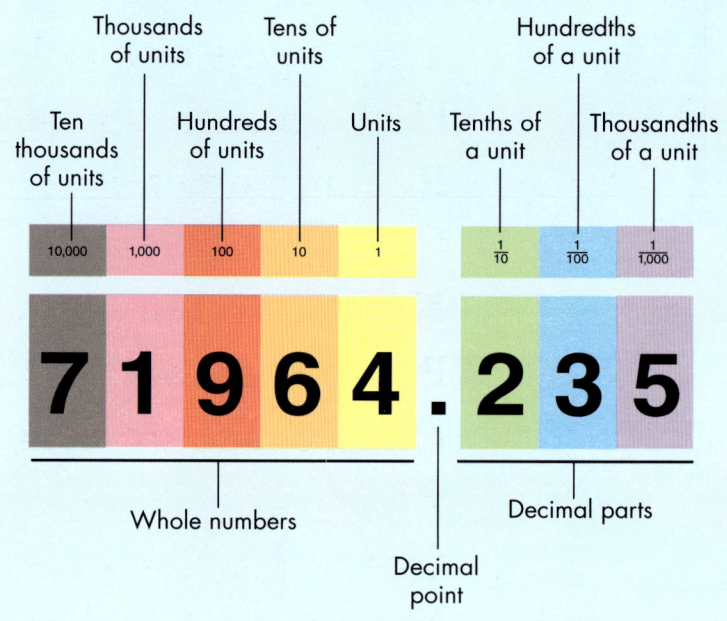

Series concept by *Brian Knapp and Duncan McCrae*
Text contributed by *Brian Knapp and Colin Bass*
Design and production by *Duncan McCrae*
Illustrations of characters by *Nicolas Debon*
Digital illustrations by *David Woodroffe*
Other illustrations by *Peter Bull Art Studio*
Editing by *Lorna Gilbert and Barbara Carragher*
Layout by *Duncan McCrae and Mark Palmer*
Reprographics by *Global Colour*
Printed and bound by *LEGO SpA, Italy*

First Published in the United States in 1999 by Grolier Educational, Sherman Turnpike, Danbury, CT 06816

Copyright © 1999
Atlantic Europe Publishing Company Limited

All rights reserved. No part of this publication may be reproduced, stored in a retrieval system, or transmitted in any form or by any means – electronic, mechanical, photocopying, recording, or otherwise – without prior permission of the Publisher.

Library of Congress Cataloging-in-Publication Data
Math Matters!
    p. cm.
    Includes indexes. .
    Contents: v.1.Numbers — v.2.Adding — v.3.Subtracting — v.4.Multiplying — v.5.Dividing — v.6.Decimals — v.7.Fractions – v.8.Shape — v.9.Size — v.10.Tables and Charts — v.11.Grids and Graphs — v.12.Chance and Average — v.13.Mental Arithmetic
    ISBN 0–7172–9294–0 (set: alk. paper). — ISBN 0–7172–9295–9 (v.1: alk. paper). — ISBN 0–7172–9296–7 (v.2: alk. paper). — ISBN 0–7172–9297–5 (v.3: alk. paper). — ISBN 0–7172–9298–3 (v.4: alk. paper). — ISBN 0–7172–9299–1 (v.5: alk. paper). — ISBN 0–7172–9300–9 (v.6: alk. paper). — ISBN 0–7172–9301–7 (v.7: alk. paper). — ISBN 0–7172–9302–5 (v.8: alk. paper). — ISBN 0–7172–9303–3 (v.9: alk. paper). — ISBN 0–7172–9304–1 (v.10: alk. paper). — ISBN 0–7172–9305–X (v.11: alk. paper). — ISBN 0–7172–9306–8 (v.12: alk. paper). — ISBN 0–7172–9307–6 (v.13: alk. paper).

    1. Mathematics — Juvenile literature. [1. Mathematics.]
I. Grolier Educational Corporation.
QA40.5.M38   1998
510 — dc21   98–7404
                                                            CIP
                                                            AC

This book is manufactured from sustainable managed forests. For every tree cut down at least one more is planted.

Contents

4	Introduction
6	The origins of numbers
8	How numerals were invented
10	Roman numerals
12	Counting systems
14	Numbers from circles
16	Putting numbers in their places
18	Using shapes for numbers
20	Zero
22	Ordered and unordered numbers
24	More than, less than, equals
26	Writing down big numbers
28	Rounded numbers
30	Minus numbers
32	Fractions and decimal numbers
34	Prime numbers
36	Numbers on graphs
38	Number patterns
40	A number triangle
42	Squares of numbers
44	What symbols mean
45	Glossary
46	Set index

Introduction

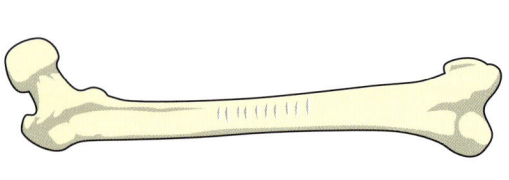

−5 < −3

Numbers are very often more important than words. They are the simplest way for people around the world to share information.

Numbers were invented thousands of years before writing. Why should this be? Because people needed numbers more urgently than letters. In fact, throughout the world many people still cannot read or write letters, but almost everyone uses numbers.

If you ever supposed that you could get by without numbers, you only need to think about money. Every country in the world has money, and many things

2, 4, 6, 8, 10, 12, 14, 16, 18, 20…

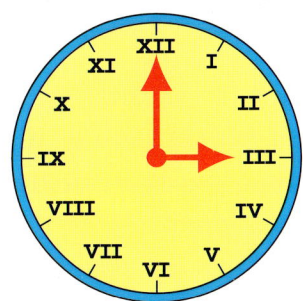

we do in everyday life involve money. It is now so common to use the symbols 0, 1, 2, 3, 4, 5, 6, 7, 8, and 9 for numbers that even in countries that do not use our alphabet, people use these common symbols for their numbers. This is why numbers are the easiest means of communication in the world today.

So, from the most ancient times, learning about numbers has been vital. And you can see why it remains so today.

There is one other thing that the world's money has in common. They use whole numbers. And that is where we start this book.

328 > 238

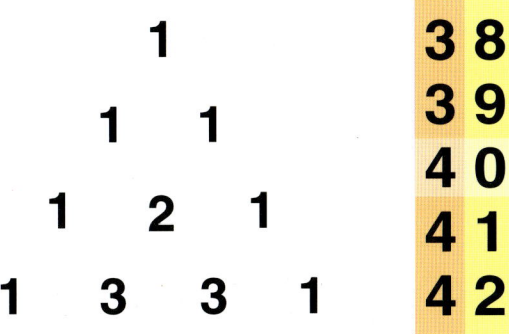

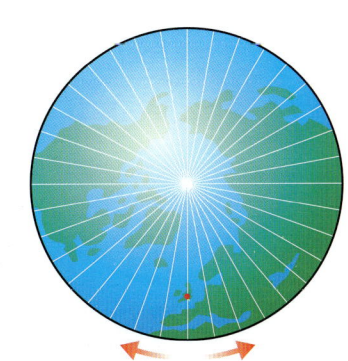

The origins of numbers

What is the simplest mathematical thing you can do with groups of objects, like bananas or cars or flowers? You can count them.

This is why the very first mathematics we learn is how to count. However, it took thousands of years for people to find a way of making symbols to count with. The earliest peoples used a bone and a piece of stone, or a twig to scratch in the ground, or pebbles.

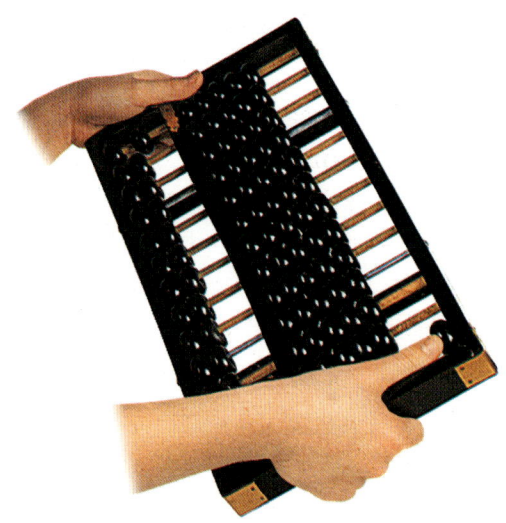

The world's oldest counting machine
This is an abacus, a system of counting based on 10 that doesn't need any symbols at all. You don't write down the answers, you just move the beads up and down the wires. In this picture the right-hand bead has been moved, meaning 1.

Using a single symbol

Suppose you choose to use pebbles or beads for counting. You put one pebble or bead on the ground to mark one thing, another one to mark two, and so on. That is, you *represent* each object by pebbles or beads. The abacus, the world's most ancient counting machine, still uses beads on a wire.

You can also make a scratch with a stone on a piece of bone, one scratch for one, another scratch next to it for two, and so on.

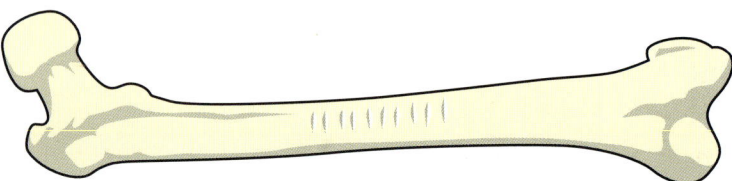

The world's oldest counting stick
The world's oldest numbers were scratched on bone. In the Stone Age people made scratches (called tallies) on bones. In this way they could keep track of, for example, the number of cattle they had. The same bones could also be used as money, a bone with ten scratches being worth twice as much as a bone with five. However, you can imagine that it would be easy to counterfeit such money, which is why ancient peoples exchanged goods rather than used scratched bones as money!

If you were living in the Stone Age and you were sending a "bone card" to your grandfather on his sixtieth birthday, using scratches you would have to write his age as:

It's not very convenient, is it? But you can easily improve on this system. If you cross every four scratches with a fifth scratch, you get little bundles of five scratches, making it easier to count larger numbers.

Now grandfather's age is shown as:

But, as you can see, this is still not a very flexible way of counting. However, it does point the way to the next stage in inventing numbers – the use of many different symbols.

Cuneiform

Getting a workable system of symbols was not that easy! The first to try were the Sumerians, Middle Eastern peoples who lived about 5,000 years ago. They used patterns of wedge-shaped symbols made with a wedge-shaped stone in wet clay. These characters are called <u>cuneiform</u>. Some of them are shown below. You can see that although they appear to use just one symbol, 10 is represented by the symbol placed horizontally. So the horizontal symbol replaces two bundles of scratches.

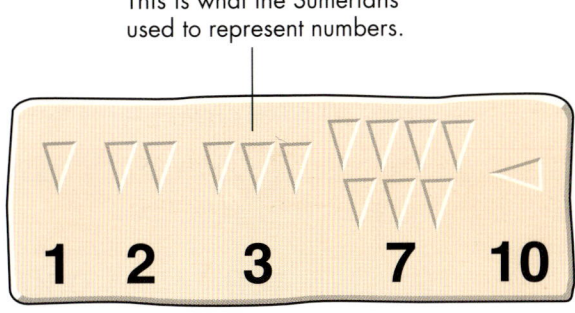

This is what the Sumerians used to represent numbers.

Remember… Numerals are symbols that represent numbers. Many people use 1, 2, 3, 4, 5, 6, 7, 8, 9, but there have been other systems as well.

Word check
Counting: Finding the total in a set of things by giving each item a number one more than the last one used.

Symbol: A mark written on paper or something else to stand for a letter, a number, or an idea of any kind.

How numerals were invented

We can say or write a number – for example, three – but when we want to use it in mathematics, we need a symbol. This symbol is called a numeral. For example, the symbol for two is the numeral **2**. Numerals, therefore, are symbols that stand for numbers.

About a thousand years after the Sumerians, the Egyptians began to use pictures instead of wedges to represent their numbers. Because it took some time to draw all these pictures, the Egyptians gradually simplified them.

The ancient Egyptians counted with symbols like those shown here. An upright stroke represented 1, a heel mark represented 10, a coiled rope represented 100, a lotus flower represented 1,000, and so on. A surprised man represented one million. We can all guess why!

▼ Ancient Egyptian symbols used for counting

Stroke	Heel mark	Coiled rope	Lotus flower	Bent finger	Tadpole (fish)	Surprised man
1	10	100	1,000	10,000	100,000	1,000,000

The Chinese used characters for numbers. Here you see three strokes for 3 and a cross for 10. But you cannot use characters to do sums, so the Chinese adopted the same system as the rest of the world.

▼ Chinese characters

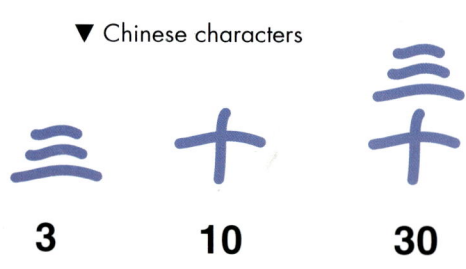

3   10   30

The Greeks and Romans used some of the letters of their alphabet as numerals. However, since the numerals and letters are the same, it is sometimes difficult to make out which is a number and which is a word!

▶ What the Greeks used

1	α	10	ι
2	β	20	κ
3	γ	30	λ
4	δ	40	μ
5	ε	50	ν
6	ς	60	ξ
7	ζ	70	ο
8	η	80	π
9	θ	90	ϟ

The Hindus of India invented a new symbol for each of the numerals.

Our modern numerals are based on these symbols invented by the Hindus of India.

This made the basis of the system that is used throughout the modern world. The original Hindu numerals were modified by the Arabs and then, over the centuries, taught to Europeans and the rest of the world. That is why we call them Arabic numerals.

Remember... The difference between numbers and numerals. A numeral is a symbol standing for a number. The Arabic numerals are: 0, 1, 2, 3, 4, 5, 6, 7, 8, 9.

Word check
Number: One or more numerals placed together represent the size of something (e.g., 45 is the numerals four and five placed together to represent the number forty-five).
Numeral: A symbol standing for a number. The modern numerals are: 0, 1, 2, 3, 4, 5, 6, 7, 8, 9. Roman numerals are I, V, X, etc.

Roman numerals

The Romans developed a set of numerals that we still use on some clocks. But you cannot do even the simplest math with it.

This was because the Romans developed a way of counting similar to that used by the Greeks – they used letters for numerals. They used capital letters such as I for **1**, V for **5**, X for **10**. So, **60** might be written:

V V V V V V V V V V V V

(which is **12** V's)

or

X X X X X X

(which is **6** X's)

But even this is hard to understand. To make it easy to read large numbers, the Romans used more capital letters: L for **50**, C for **100** (that's where "cents" came from!), D for **500** and M for **1,000**. In this way VI is six, VII is seven, VIII is eight, but VIIII is not nine. For numbers just below ten, the Romans took **1** from **10** by putting the I in front of the X like this: IX.

As a result, the **6** in the numbers shown below is represented by two different symbols depending on the size of the whole number:

604 is DCIV

69 is LXIX

This is how they organized their numerals. If the same symbol is repeated to the right (for example, XX), then it means add (in this case **10 + 10**, which is **20**). When a symbol is found to the left of a symbol that has a bigger value (for example, IX) then it means take away (in this case X (**10**) − I (**1**), which is **9**).

This was not a flexible system for doing the mathematics needed in everyday life. So it gradually died out, except for specialized uses.

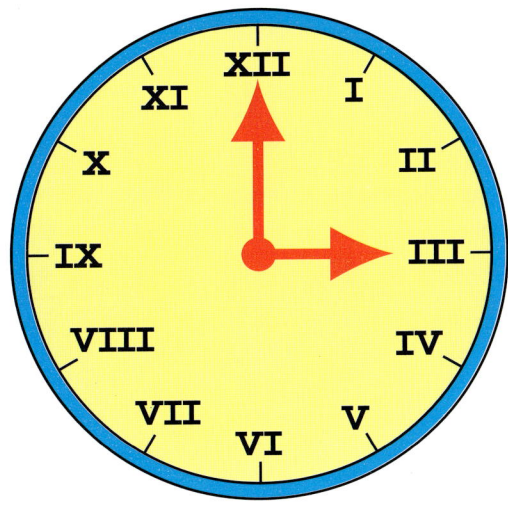
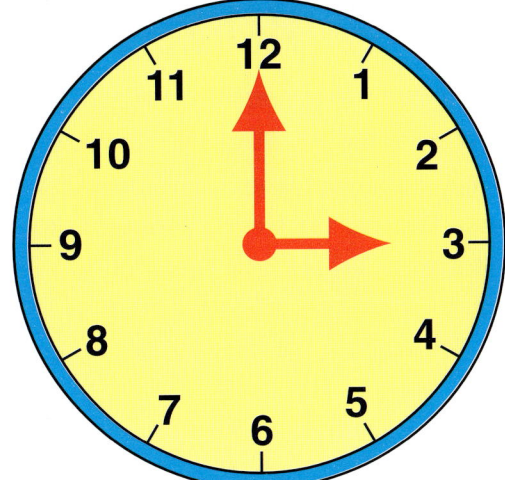

Roman time

The hours on a clock are sometimes marked off using Roman numerals. But there is nothing useful in this. It is simply that Roman numerals look more decorative on some types of clock face.

In case you have to read Roman numerals, the picture above and the table on the left shows what the Roman numerals look like, compared to the modern numerals.

Dates

Sometimes people still use the Roman numeral system for dates. Since I=1, V=5, X=10, L=50, C=100, D=500, and M=1,000, MCMXCVIII is 1998, and MMV is the year 2005.

Remember... Roman numerals are based on a system of **10**. Numbers are built up from combinations of I, V, X, L, C, D, and M.

1	I
2	II
3	III
4	IV
5	V
6	VI
7	VII
8	VIII
9	IX
10	X
11	XI
12	XII

Counting systems

We use three systems for counting. The first is based on **10** (for everyday counting); the second is based on **60** (for circles), and the third is based on **2** (for computers).

Numbers based on 10

Using a finger system makes it easy to understand why we use numbers based on **10**. The ten numerals are also called digits. Digit is a word that comes from the Latin word for "finger."

We can combine digits to make larger numbers by putting them side by side, such as **237**. But there are rules to this, as you will see on page 16.

Numbers based on 60

It may be convenient to count in **10**'s, but about **5,000** years ago the Babylonians, who lived in the region that is now the country of Iraq, developed a system of numbers based on **60**. So all their numbers were grouped into **60**'s.

We still use this system for some very important things. For example, each hour has **60** minutes, and each minute has **60** seconds. A circle is also divided into **60**'s. There are six **60**'s, or **360** degrees, in a circle.

Circular system

The system based on circles uses **60** as its main unit. In fact, a circle is made up of **360** degrees. Half a circle is therefore **180** degrees, and a quarter of a circle is **90** degrees. When the circle tells the time, a whole circle is **12** hours, **6** hours is a half circle, and **3** hours is a quarter circle. One minute is a **60**th of a circle $^{360}/_{60}$, or **6** degrees. One hour is a **12**th of a circle, or **30** degrees ($^{360}/_{12}$).

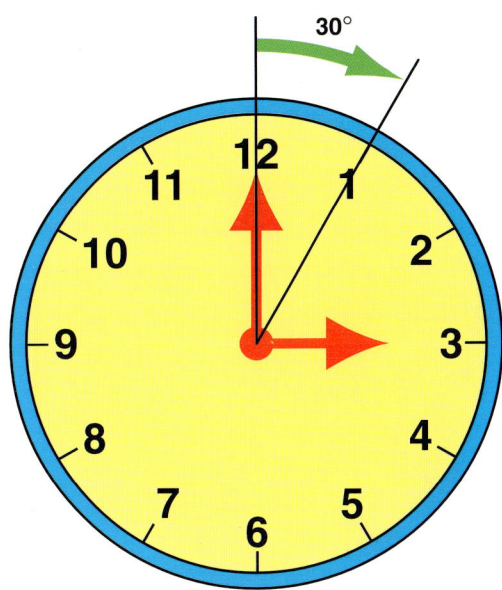

Book link... Find out more about degrees on the next page in this book and in the book *Size* in the *Math Matters!* set.

Numbers based on 2

What good is it to have just two numerals? Not much – unless you are a computer. Computers are simply very fast switches that switch on and off, that is, they switch between 1 and 0. Computers get away with being so dumb because they are very, very fast!

10	=	**2**
100	=	**4**
101	=	**5**
1010	=	**10**
111100	=	**60**

Remember... The two hands on a clock use the markings on the clock differently. The hour hand uses the numerals marked on the clock. The minute hand uses the little marks in between them.

Word check

Circle: A loop whose boundary is the same distance from the center all the way around.

Degree: A small part of a complete turn. There are 360 degrees in a complete turn.

Digit: The numerals 1, 2, 3, 4, 5, 6, 7, 8, 9, or 0. Several may be used to stand for a larger number.

Numbers from circles

If you stand with your arms outstretched and swivel on the spot, your arms trace out a complete circle. The hands of a watch make a complete turn as they sweep from twelve back all the way to twelve.

Even ancient peoples like the Babylonians knew about circles, and they made up a number system to use with them. It was based on the number 60. They split up a circle into 360 equal parts. In geometry each one of these parts is called a degree.

Finding our way around the world

If we look at the earth from the North or South pole, it is circular. The Equator is the imaginary circle round the earth halfway between the North and South Poles. The earth is divided into 360 degrees called degrees of longitude.

Greenwich in London is the agreed starting point for this system. Places west of Greenwich are given a longitude angle measuring how far around the earth you must travel to reach them. For example, Washington, DC, is 77 degrees west. Sydney, Australia, is 151 degrees east.

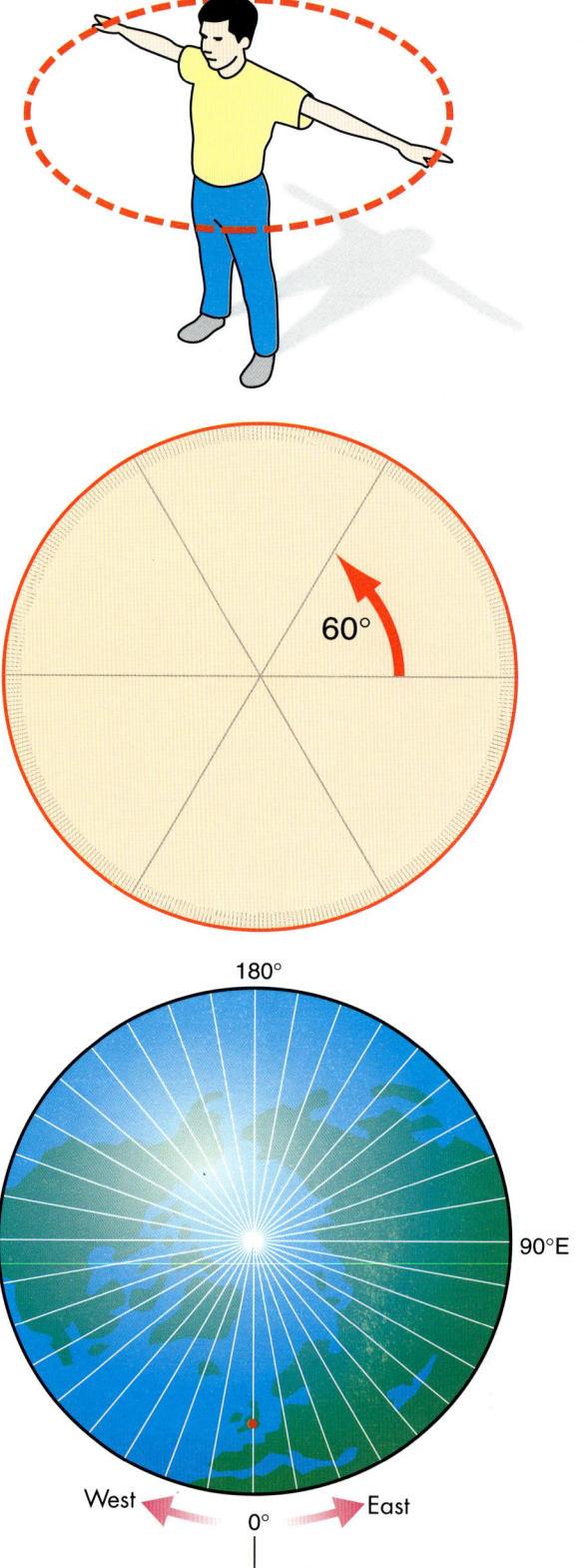

14

Clocks

Clocks also measure a circle, as you have seen on page 12. Measuring on a clock begins at the top of the circle for historical reasons. Every day the sun is at its highest halfway between sunrise and sunset. We call this noon.

An hour is made up of **60** smaller numbers called minutes; a minute is made up of **60** smaller parts called seconds. So, even though these are smaller parts, they are still whole numbers.

Circle numbers: pi

Pi stands for a special number connected to circles. The boundary (circumference) of a circle is the distance across it (diameter) × pi.

Pi is roughly 3$\frac{1}{7}$ or $\frac{22}{7}$. As a decimal, pi is approximately **3.142**.

Book link... Find our more about circles and pi in the books *Shape* and *Size* in the *Math Matters!* set.

Find out about mixed numbers and improper fractions in the book *Fractions* in the *Math Matters!* set.

Find out about decimals in the book *Decimals* in the *Math Matters!* set.

Remember... The most common use for circle numbers is degrees. The earth makes a complete turn every 24 hours. That is $\frac{360}{24}$, which is **15** degrees an hour. So every **1** hour time zone is **15** degrees of longitude further around the world.

Word check

Degree: A small part of a complete turn. There are 360 degrees in a complete turn.

Longitude: Angles that mark the distance of places east or west of Greenwich.

Pole: The North and South Poles are the two points on the earth's surface around which the earth spins.

Time zone: A band of the earth sharing the same time. Time zones vary with longitude.

Putting numbers in their places

Numbers are made from numerals built up from the <u>right</u>, so that we always know how big they are.

This modern system of numbers is very useful because you cannot mistake what has been written down. Every number has its place, and the place you put each number tells you many things about it.

Some numbers use just one numeral, or digit, like this:

8 (meaning eight of something).

But most numbers use more than one numeral, or digit, like this:

38 (meaning thirty-eight of something)

or

238 (meaning two hundred and thirty-eight of something)

Notice how the digits are placed in a special order to make a number. The digit with the smallest value (units) in a whole number is always on the right. This is a rule that we usually take for granted, but it is vitally important!

If we place the numerals in **238** in a different order, we get different numbers:

328 is three hundred and twenty-eight.

832 is eight hundred and thirty-two.

You use the same rule for really large numbers, such as **299,792,458**, which is how many meters light travels in just one second.

These columns help show the numbers described on the left of this page.

Hundreds of units	Tens of units	Units
		8
	3	8
2	3	8
3	2	8
8	3	2

Where you place a numeral shows its value

You can see here how placing a number correctly works. A whole number is built up from the right. A number up to 9 goes on the right. Then, to the left of this, a single numeral is used to show the tens from 10 to 90, another single numeral to the left of this shows the hundreds from 100 to 900, and so on.

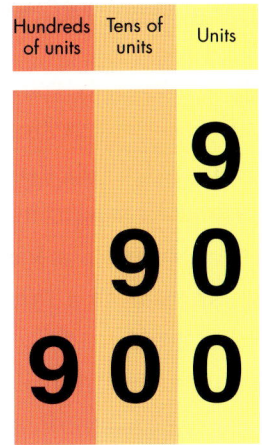

Using columns to keep numerals in their places

It is often helpful to think of numbers as being placed in "hidden" columns. Throughout the *Math Matters!* set of books we will often show the hidden columns using colors. They will be used as guides to make calculations such as adding, subtracting, multiplying, and dividing easier. The way the columns are used is shown on the right and on page 2.

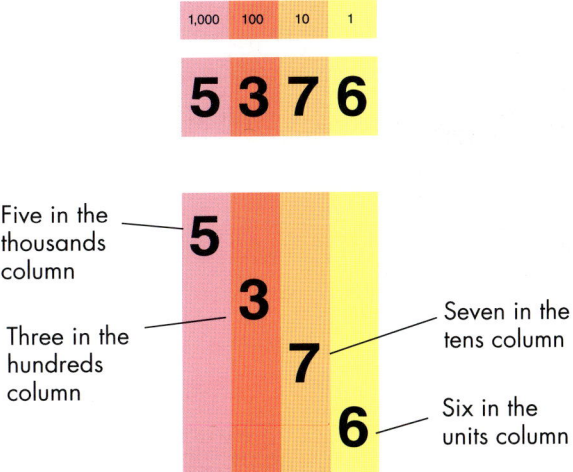

This number, 5,376, is five thousand three hundred and seventy-six. The value of each number is shown above.

Remember... Place values. Mathematicians often talk of "place value," meaning the value of a numeral because of its place in a number. So, a 5 put 3 places from the right in a number like 3,567 has a value of 500.

Word check
Place: The way we arrange numerals so that we know the value of a digit in a number.

Whole number: A number containing only complete units, not parts of units (it does not contain decimals or fractions).

Using shapes for numbers

Some people find that they work with pictures of numbers in their head. The shapes shown below may help you do this, too.

Here, you can see a single unit as a small square, ten units shown as a long shape and a hundred units shown as a large square shape, or "flat" shape.

We can now use these shapes (which are each 10 times bigger or smaller than their neighbor) to see how numbers are made up.

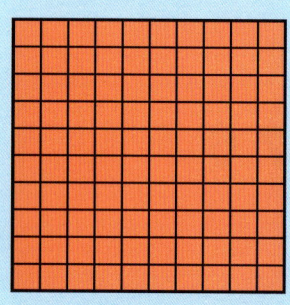 ◀ This is a shape for 100. You can prove this by counting up all 100 squares, or units, if you like. Some people call this shape a <u>flat</u>.

◀ This is a shape for 10. Some people call this a <u>long</u>. Ten longs make a flat.

◀ This is a shape for 1. It can also be called a <u>unit</u>. 10 units make a long.

Using models makes it very easy to see which of two numbers is bigger. Below we show what **238** looks like. Compare it to **328** on the opposite page.

Hundreds of units	Tens of units	Units
2	**3**	**8**

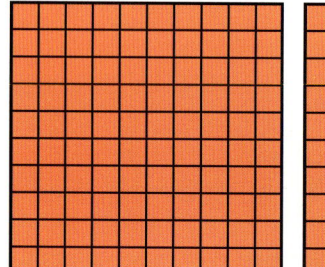 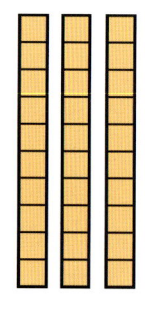

200
2 flats

30
3 longs

8
8 units

18

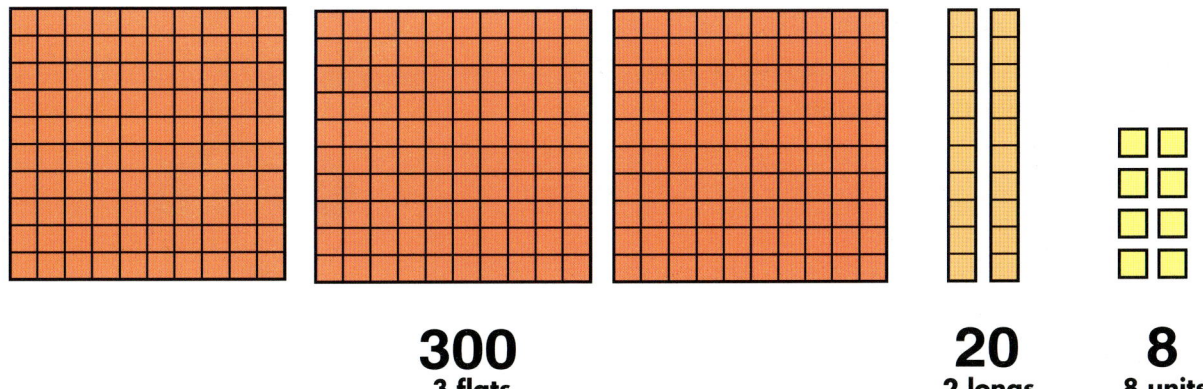

300
3 flats

20
2 longs

8
8 units

The number **328** has three flats. A number that has only two flats cannot possibly be as big as a number with three flats however many longs and units it has. This is because the greatest number of longs allowed is **9**, worth **90** altogether, and the greatest number of units is **9** also, making the total value of longs and flats **99**, one less than the value of a flat. So **328** must be bigger than **238**.

Remember… Models can help you see the relative sizes of numbers.

Word check
Flat: A large square representing 100. It can also be made up of ten "longs" put side by side.
Long: A long shape representing 10.
Unit: 1 of something. A small, square shape representing 1.

Zero

Zero, which means "none," or "nil," was the last numeral to be invented. It was needed to help count in tens.

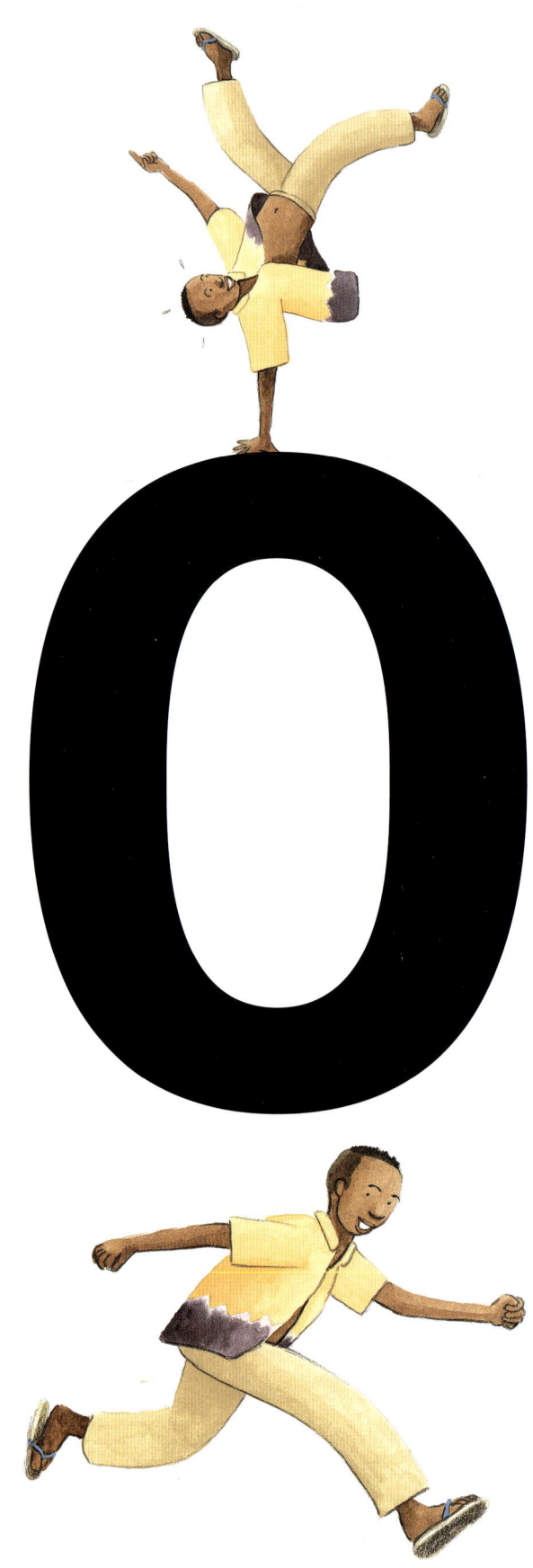

The original Hindu-Arab way of writing numerals is very close to the system we all use today (see page 9). But to begin with, only 9 numerals were invented. Until about a thousand years ago there was no symbol for zero (0). This made it very difficult to write a symbol for 10 or 100. So why didn't they mind?

The Hindu-Arabs didn't use the zero because they couldn't think why you would need a symbol to represent nothing. And because it was nothing, they just left a gap. Of course, this could be very confusing. Is "2 " just two or twenty (20) or two hundred (200)?

Indeed, as we know, some "nothings" are very important. For example, you couldn't be a millionaire unless you had six "nothings" to put after the 1!

When zero has a "value"

When you count things in a set, you count up one at a time, like this: "one, two, three, four, five," and so on.

But when you count down one at a time, you can include a zero, like this: "five, four, three, two, one, zero." This is because it is sometimes important to know that you have nothing left.

Using zero in a number

The Romans would have written one hundred and three as "CIII." Using the original Hindu-Arabic system, which separates numbers into units, tens, hundreds, and so on, this would have been written as:

They did not have a symbol for 0. It looks all right here because we are using our colored columns to hold each number in its proper place, but if we took these away, it would not be easy to tell 103 from 13:

1   3

1 3

To keep the 1 and the 3 apart, and to avoid confusion with 13, zero was invented.

We do the same thing when we want to hold the places at the end of a number to show how big it is. For example, the 0 is used in 10 to hold the place of no units.

Similarly, 0's are used in 1,000 to hold the place of no hundreds, no tens, and no units.

1 0 0 0

You cannot, however, count zero things. The counting numbers begin at one. Zero is not a counting number, it is a place-holding number.

Remember... Zero simply fills up a place when there is nothing else to put in it. For example, no tens, no units. It is not a counting number.

Word check
Set: A collection of things we are interested in.

Did you know? The ancient Greek mathematicians were very good at working with shapes (geometry). But because zero hadn't been invented, they made hardly any progress with the mathematics of number (arithmetic).

Ordered and unordered numbers

When we count a set of things, the order in which we tick them off does not matter. When the order does matter, however, we use special number words such as "first" and write numbers such as "1st" instead of 1.

Counting for a race

Six athletes are going to run a race. When the starter tells them to line up at the start line, they each stand next to a running lane, and the lanes are marked with numbers 1, 2, 3, 4, 5, 6. It does not matter which athlete stands in which lane or in which order the starter counts them. Their order is unimportant because the starter simply needs to know that there are six runners. These are therefore called unordered numbers.

As they finish the race, each runner is given a little card. On one side the winner's card says "First," and on the other side it says "1st." The next runner to finish the race is given a card saying "Second" and "2nd." The others, in the order in which they finish, are given cards saying "Third" and "3rd," "Fourth" and "4th," "Fifth" and "5th," and "Sixth" and "6th." The order now matters very much, so they are known as ordered numbers.

Ordered and unordered numbers

In the ordered numbers notice the "-th" pattern from fourth onward. The first three ordered numbers don't fit this or any pattern. Notice also that "fifth," "eighth," and "ninth" are harder to spell than the others.

Every unordered (also called "cardinal") number, however big, has an ordered (also called "ordinal") number to go with it, made by using the "-th" pattern.

Remember... Use unordered numbers such as 1, 2, 3, and so on for numbers where the order does not matter, and ordered words, such as first, second, and so on, when the order is important.

▼ Chart of ordered numbers

Ordered numbers	
1st	first
2nd	second
3rd	third
4th	fourth
5th	fifth
6th	sixth
7th	seventh
8th	eighth
9th	ninth
10th	tenth

▼ Chart of unordered numbers

Unordered numbers	
1	one
2	two
3	three
4	four
5	five
6	six
7	seven
8	eight
9	nine
10	ten

Word check

Ordered numbers: Numbers used for putting things in order, such as first, second, third, fourth, fifth, and so on. Also called "ordinal numbers."

Unordered numbers: Numbers used for counting when the order does not matter, such as one, two, three, four, five, and so on. Also called "cardinal numbers" or "counting numbers."

More than, less than, equals

Mathematicians have special short-cut symbols for writing "more than" or "less than." They are often combined with the symbol for equals, as you will see below.

More than and less than

The special symbol for "is bigger than" is >. So we can write "three hundred and twenty-eight is bigger than two hundred and thirty-eight" entirely in mathematical symbols like this:

328 > 238

The same number sentence can also be written the other way around:

238 < 328

In this case the < symbol means "is smaller than" (two hundred and thirty-eight is less than three hundred and twenty-eight).

Notice that the wider end of the symbol is next to the bigger number.

This is just as true for big numbers, so that:

239,000 < 239,001

Notice that this works even when one number is just 1 unit bigger than the other.

Using more than or less than with equals

When two numbers are the same, we use the = (equals) symbol.

Sometimes, we can combine the <, >, and = symbols. For example, if you travel internationally by air, you might find that your baggage allowance is put like this:

Free baggage allowance  20 kg

This means that if your bags weigh less than 20 kg, they are free, and if their weight equals 20 kg, they are still free.

Another way to write this would be to use a > sign. In this case you would see that bags are charged if their weight > 20 kg.

Between

Here is a way of writing that a value must be between two numbers.

In a science experiment the instructions might state that the experiment must be done between the temperatures of 20°C and 23°C. In which case it could be written as:

$$20°C \leq \text{temperature} \leq 23°C$$

As you can see, you can use the symbols, <, ≤, =, ≥, and > to give some very precise instructions.

Remember... When you see this symbol >, the arrow points to the <u>smaller</u> number.

Word check

Equation: A number sentence using the = symbol, telling us that two different ways of writing a number are the same. For example, 2 + 2 = 4 and 9 − 5 = 4.

Ordering: Putting numbers in order of size, for which the symbols < and > are very useful.

Writing down big numbers

Sometimes it is helpful to place numbers as though they were on top of hidden or colored columns. Big numbers, however, can pose some special problems, and so we need to use another way.

Here is how to write them down more easily.

Look first at how big numbers are related:

Ten tens make one hundred	100
Ten hundreds make one thousand	1,000
Ten thousands make ten thousand	10,000
Ten ten-thousands make one hundred thousand	100,000
Ten hundred-thousands make one million	1,000,000
Ten millions make ten million	10,000,000
Ten ten-millions make one hundred million	100,000,000
Ten hundred-millions make one billion	1,000,000,000
Ten billions make ten billion	10,000,000,000
Ten ten-billions make one hundred billion	100,000,000,000
Ten hundred-billions make one trillion	1,000,000,000,000

But you can see that most of the room is taken up holding the size with zeros.

When we have a number with zeros, we can write it down in a shorthand form. We have already used one way above. We call numbers with two 0's behind them "hundreds," those with three 0's "thousands" and so on.

But there is another way that can be very useful. We count up the number of zeros (which represent tens) and put this number above and to the right of the **10** like this:

10	can be written	10^1
100	can be written	10^2
1,000	can be written	10^3
10,000	can be written	10^4
100,000	can be written	10^5
1,000,000	can be written	10^6
10,000,000	can be written	10^7
100,000,000	can be written	10^8
1,000,000,000	can be written	10^9
10,000,000,000	can be written	10^{10}
100,000,000,000	can be written	10^{11}
1,000,000,000,000	can be written	10^{12}

10^2 — means (10×10)
10^3 — means $(10 \times 10 \times 10)$

Remember… How big numbers are spoken: 10^2 is said as "ten squared," and 10^3 is said as "ten cubed." But 10^4 is said as "ten to the power of four" or just "ten to the fourth." This also applies to larger powers.

Word check
Powers: Little symbols written above the line, like the 4 in 10^4.

Did you know? The number of ways of rearranging the **13** volumes in this series along a bookshelf is $13 \times 12 \times 11 \times 10 \times 9 \times 8 \times 7 \times 6 \times 5 \times 4 \times 3 \times 2$, which is more than 1 billion (1 followed by **9** zeros). The number of ways of rearranging a deck of **52** playing cards is nearly 10 followed by **68** zeros!

Rounded numbers

A rounded number is a whole number that ends in one or more zero's.

A rounded number is useful when we do not need a very exact answer, such as when we want to remember something or simply get a general idea. Someone might ask: "Give me a rough idea of how many bricks I will need to build this wall." Another word often used instead of "rough idea" is "estimate."

For example, if we were traveling in a car and someone asked the speed, the driver may answer: "About 40." The actual speed may have been 38, 39, 40, 41, or 42, but 40 was good enough to get a general idea of speed.

To find a rounded number

Look at the last digit. If it is less than 5, throw it away and replace it with 0. If it is 5 or more, then add 1 to the next digit left, then throw away the last digit and replace it with 0.

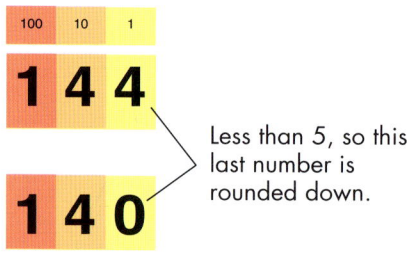

Less than 5, so this last number is rounded down.

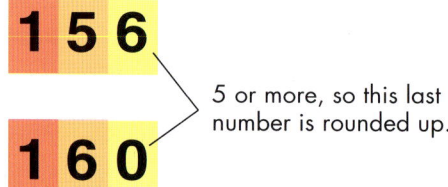

5 or more, so this last number is rounded up.

You can repeat the rounding process in the tens column.

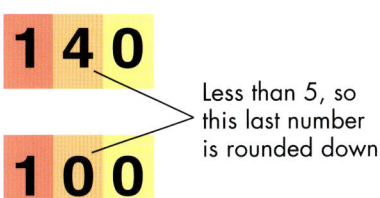
Less than 5, so this last number is rounded down.

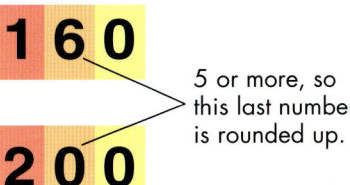
5 or more, so this last number is rounded up.

We call this process rounding off. If the answer gets smaller, we sometimes talk about rounding down, and about rounding up when the answer gets bigger as a result of our rounding.

Notice that each time we round, the number gets less accurate, so we have to be careful to round only as much as is needed.

Also… It is better to round two or more places in one go. For example, 146 rounds off to 100 not to 200.

Remember… Rounding produces numbers that are easier to work with but less accurate.

Word check
Significant figures: The numbers (reading from the left) that you need for your purpose. This is a way of describing how precise the number is. It is not affected by the position of the decimal point, which has more to do with the units being used.
Rounding: Making a number shorter.

Minus numbers

Numbers placed in line make a scale. Scales can include ordinary (positive) numbers as well as zero and minus (negative), numbers.

If you want to know the temperature in your room, you use a thermometer. We can easily read the temperature by looking at the numbers next to the tube.

When we put numbers in a line, we make a scale. The distance between the numbers is always the same.

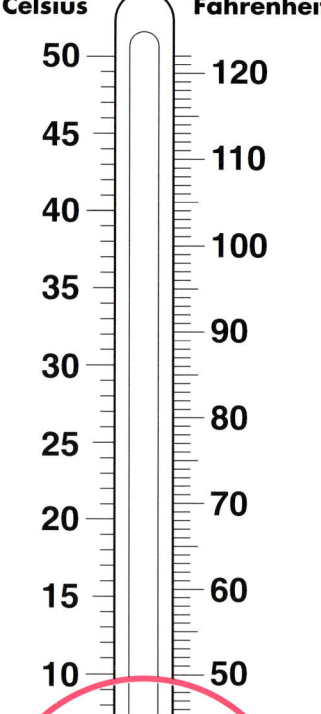

A cold night

As the temperature falls in a greenhouse on a cold winter night, Mr. Young's plants might be damaged.

The Celsius (°C) scale on the thermometer includes zero. Although you cannot count zero things, a temperature of zero is real enough.

The temperature has been falling in equal steps. Zero is as much below one as one is below two.

Zero °C is the temperature at which ice forms. If the night is cold enough, the temperature could go on falling. What could be below zero? The answer is written down using minus numbers.

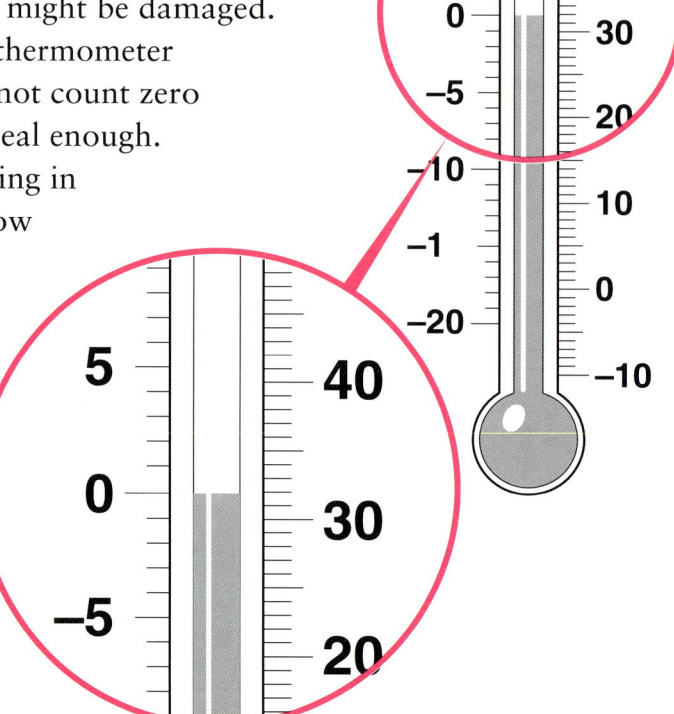

If the temperature continued to fall in equal steps, we would count them down like this: minus one, minus two, minus three, and so on.

Minus numbers are written using the "−" symbol, which is also used for subtraction. Thus "minus three" is written as "−3."

A temperature of −5 is colder than a temperature of −3. In mathematical symbols this would be written:

$$-5 < -3$$

Remember... How minus numbers are said. Most people say, for example, −3 as "minus three."

Word check

− : Between two numbers the symbol means "subtract" or "minus." In front of one number it means the number is a minus number. In Latin *minus* means "less."

Minus numbers: The numbers that fall below zero on a number line (scale). Minus numbers or zero cannot be used for counting, only for measuring things like temperature. Minus numbers are also called negative numbers.

Book link... Find out more about how to use minus numbers, and about the '−' symbol, in the book *Subtracting* in the *Math Matters!* set.

Fractions and decimal numbers

Fractions and decimals show how something has been split into parts. We use them when we want to split up a whole number into parts.

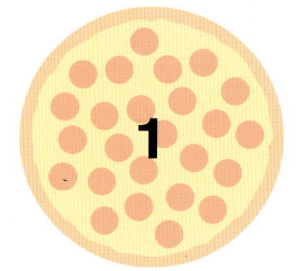

This is 1 complete pizza. Think of it as 1 part of 1 pizza.

Fractions

A fraction is one number above the other with a horizontal dividing line between them. The number on the bottom of the fraction tells us how many equal parts the original was broken into. If the fraction is

$$\frac{1}{5}$$

then the original 1 was broken into 5 equal pieces.

We call the number on the bottom of the fraction the denominator.

The number on the top of the fraction tells us how many of those parts we have.

If the fraction is

$$\frac{2}{5}$$

then we have 2 of the original 5 pieces. We call the number on the top of the fraction the numerator.

Fractions are the most useful kind of number when we want to show that we have broken things up equally. We use many fraction words every day for just this purpose. For example, we say we have a half, three-quarters, a quarter, an eighth, and so on. You can see this with the pizza example on the right.

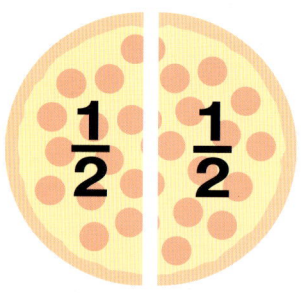

The pizza has been split equally so that it makes 2 equal portions. The 1 pizza is now in 2 equal parts. Each is part of the 1 and is written as:

$$\frac{1}{2}$$

— The number of portions each person has.
— The total number of portions.

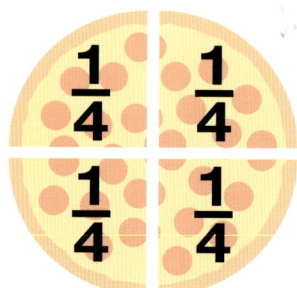

The pizza has now been split equally so that it makes 4 equal portions. Each is part of the 1 and is written as:

$$\frac{1}{4}$$

Decimals

In a decimal number whole numbers are written to the left of the decimal point and part numbers to the right.

To write a decimal, we simply put a mathematician's period (called a decimal point) after the end of the whole numbers and <u>carry on to the right</u>.

Just as with whole numbers, which have the smallest value on the right and the largest on the left, so every number to the right of the decimal point has a value ten times smaller than its left-hand neighbor. So the further it is to the right, the smaller its value. Numbers to the right of units are described as tenths, hundredths, thousandths, and so on.

$$3\;4\;7 = 347$$

$$3\;4\;7\;.\;5 = 347 + \frac{5}{10}$$

$$3\;4\;7\;.\;5\;8 = 347 + \frac{58}{100}$$

Remember... Fractions and decimals are used to describe parts of numbers.

Book link... Find out more about fractions, and about how to add and subtract them, from the book *Fractions* in the *Math Matters!* set. You can also find out more about decimals in the book *Decimals* in the *Math Matters!* set.

Word check

Decimal point: A dot written after the units when a number contains parts of a unit as well as whole numbers.

Denominator: The number written on the bottom of a fraction.

Numerator: The number written on the top of a fraction.

Prime numbers

Some numbers of objects can be arranged in several neat rows. Prime numbers can be arranged in only one way.

Anisa's butterfly collection

Anisa had a collection of photographs of butterflies, which she enjoyed arranging in different ways.

When she had 24, she could arrange them like this:

4 × 6

or like this:

8 × 3

or like this:

12 × 2

Still, that was better than when she previously had only 23 butterflies. Then she could only arrange them in a boring row 23 long, or in rows of unequal length, or in a heap.

23 × 1

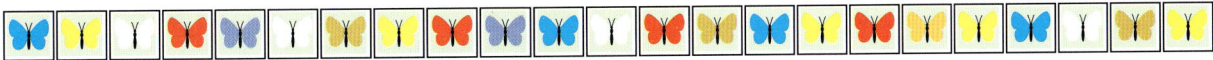

Numbers that can be arranged into neat rows all of the same length are called multiples. The number 24 is a multiple of 2, 3, 4, 6, 8, and 12 because they are the numbers of rows you can use (you will need to turn some of the diagrams around to see this).

A number such as 23, which can only have one row of 23 (or 23 rows of 1), is called a prime number. There are lots of prime numbers. The ones below 23 are: 2, 3, 5, 7, 11, 13, 17, and 19.

The other whole numbers less than 23 are multiples. There are, of course, lots of bigger multiples and prime numbers too!

Remember... A prime number cannot be divided by any other number, except 1.

Word check
Multiple: A number of objects that can be rearranged into several rows of equal length and longer than just one.

Prime number: A number that is not a multiple of anything (2, 3, 5, 7, 11, 13, 17, 19, etc., are prime numbers).

Numbers on graphs

A graph is a way of showing the connection between pairs of numbers.

Numbers can often be made easier to understand by turning them into pictures. One form of mathematical picture is called a graph.

Here, for example, is a table of numbers showing the temperature of the air through a day. The temperature was measured at midnight, 4 a.m., 8 a.m. and so on in four-hour intervals. The temperature was measured in degrees Celsius (°C).

It is not very easy to see exactly what is going on from this table, which is why it is helpful to make a picture, or graph.

▼ **Chart of the temperature of the air through the day**

Time (24-hour clock)	Temperature °C
0 (midnight)	4
4 (a.m.)	2
8 (a.m.)	8
12 (noon)	12
16 (4 p.m.)	12
20 (8 p.m.)	8
24 (midnight)	4

Making a line graph

The kind of graph we want is called a line graph. When we have finished all of the readings in the table, they will be shown on the graph and connected by a line.

Step 1: First we need two scales to start to build our picture. One scale (which measures time) will go across the bottom of our picture; the other scale (which measures temperature) will go up the left-hand side of our picture.

Notice that we have drawn the scales on a grid of lines. Paper with grids of lines like this is called graph paper, and it makes it easier to place numbers accurately.

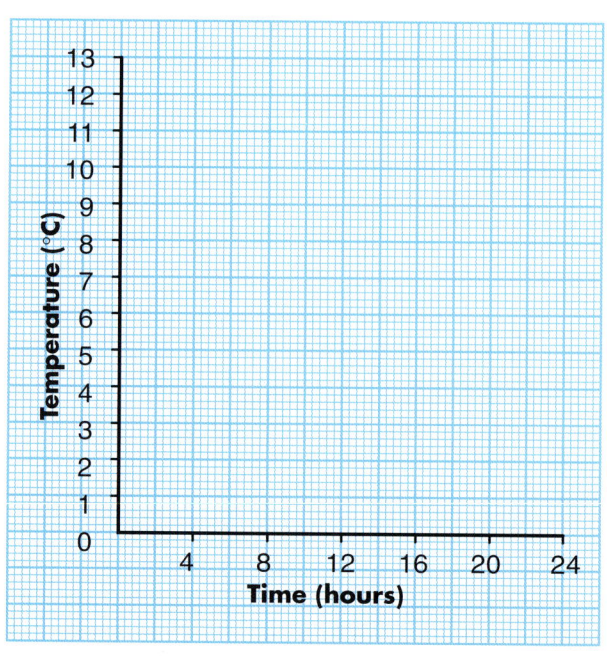

Book link... For more information on plotting graphs see the book *Grids and graphs* in the *Math Matters!* set.

Step 2: Graphs use pairs of numbers. Each pair of numbers is called a pair of coordinates.

See how the numbers in the table opposite have been grouped together to make coordinates in the table on this page. The numbers have been placed together, separated by a comma, and put in brackets like this:

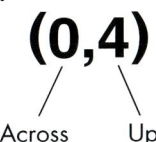

Across Up

▼ **Chart of the temperature of the air through the day**

Time (24-hour clock)	Temperature °C	Coordinates
0 (midnight)	4	(0,4)
4 (a.m.)	2	(4,2)
8 (a.m.)	8	(8,8)
12 (noon)	12	(12,12)
16 (4 p.m.)	12	(16,12)
20 (8 p.m.)	8	(20,8)
24 (midnight)	4	(24,4)

Step 3: Next we plot the coordinates. To plot (16,12) we first go across 16 on the scale and then up 12. We draw a dot and place the coordinates beside it. All the other numbers are plotted in the same way.

Step 4: Join the points with a line.

▼ **Graph of the temperature of the air through the day**

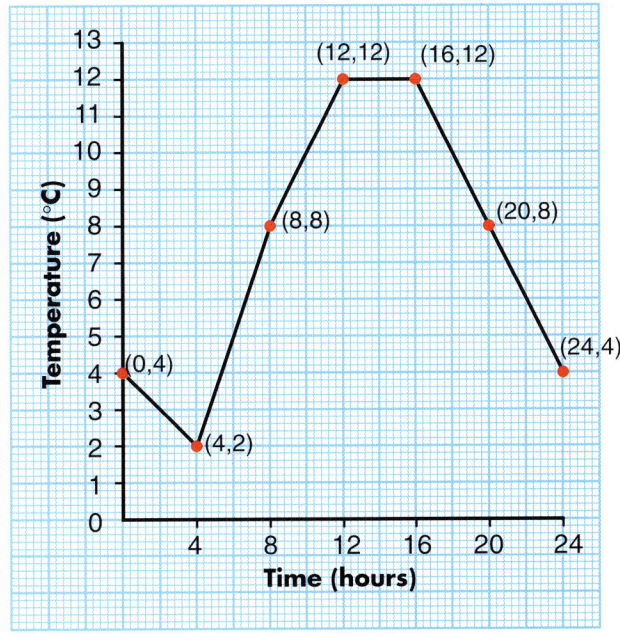

Remember... Numbers can often be made easier to understand when they are drawn as pictures, such as line graphs.

Word check

Coordinates: The pair of numbers that tells you the position of a point on a graph. They are usually enclosed with parentheses.

Line graph: A graph on which a line is drawn through a set of points.

Scale: A set of marks on a line used for measuring.

Number patterns

Numbers can be found in many patterns. The simplest patterns are the numbers we have already used. For example:

These three dots mean that the pattern continues.

Counting numbers:

1, 2, 3, 4, 5, 6, 7, 8, 9, 10, 11…

Even numbers:

2, 4, 6, 8, 10, 12, 14, 16, 18, 20…

Odd numbers:

1, 3, 5, 7, 9, 11, 13, 15, 17, 19, 21…

Multiples: for example multiples of 3:

3, 6, 9, 12, 15, 18, 21, 24… (your 3 times table)

Multiples of 7:

7, 14, 21, 28, 35, 42, 49, 56, 63… (your 7 times table)

Prime numbers:

2, 3, 5, 7, 9, 11, 13…

You will find triangular and square patterns on pages 40 and 42.

Rules for patterns

Patterns of numbers always follow rules. For example, counting numbers follow the rule:

> Add 1 to the previous number to get the next number.

There are many interesting patterns, but they may not seem like patterns unless you know the rule. For example:

> Start with 1, 2. Each new number is formed by adding the two numbers before it.
> Thus the number after 1, 2 is 1 + 2 = 3
> The pattern is now 1, 2, 3.

1 + 2 = 3

> Using the rule, the next number is 2 + 3 = 5
> The pattern is now 1, 2, 3, 5.

2 + 3 = 5

> Using the rule, the next number is 3 + 5 = 8
> The pattern is now 1, 2, 3, 5, 8... and so on.

3 + 5 = 8

Here is another pattern produced by a simple rule:

> Start with 1, 2. Each new number is formed by multiplying the two numbers before it.
> Thus the number after 1, 2 is 1 × 2 = 2
> The pattern is now 1, 2, 2

1 × 2 = 2

> The next number is 2 × 2 = 4
> The pattern is now 1, 2, 2, 4.

2 × 2 = 4

> The next number is 2 × 4 = 8
> The pattern is now 1, 2, 2, 4, 8... and so on.

2 × 4 = 8

You can easily produce more of these patterns for yourself. Try including subtracting and dividing as well.

Remember... Numbers often occur in patterns, even if this is not obvious until you know the rule that produced them.

A number triangle

Here are some patterns that make triangles. Each triangle is made of numbers that contain dozens more patterns.

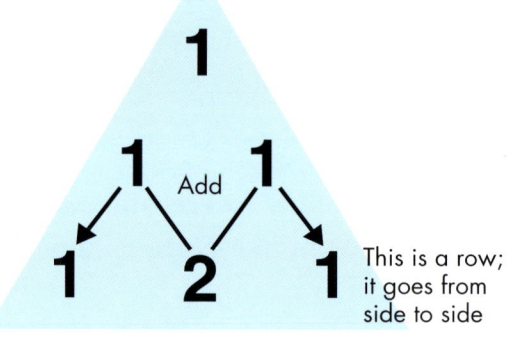

This is a row; it goes from side to side

Look to see how this pattern is made. All the rows begin and end with 1. Each of the other numbers is found by adding the two closest numbers in the row above.

This triangle of numbers can be made any size you want. The biggest one shown here has 11 rows.

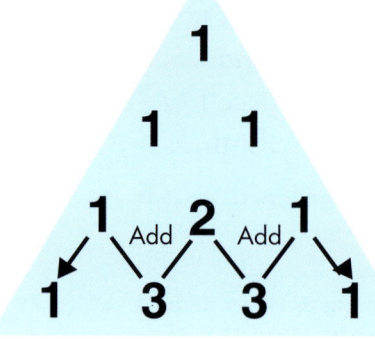

Notice some more patterns:
The outside sloping sides are all ones. The next sloping row from the edge is made up of the counting numbers 1, 2, 3, and so on. You can probably find many other patterns, too.

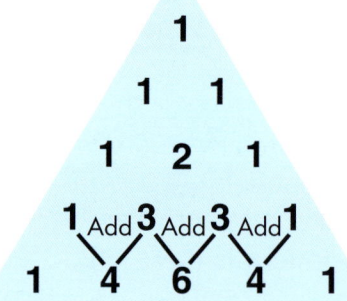

```
                    1
                  1   1
                1   2   1
              1   3   3   1
            1   4   6   4   1
          1   5  10  10   5   1
        1   6  15  20  15   6   1
      1   7  21  35  35  21   7   1
    1   8  28  56  70  56  28   8   1
  1   9  36  84 126 126  84  36   9   1
1  10  45 120 210 252 210 120  45  10   1
```

Arranging things in triangles

Tom had a collection of shells and arranged them like this.

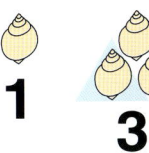
1

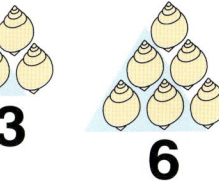
3

6

10

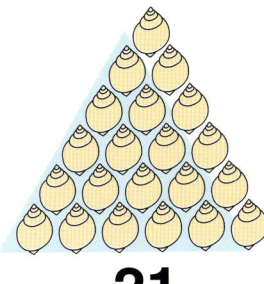
15

21

Count the number of shells in each triangle. Quite apart from the pattern of the triangles, there is a pattern in the numbers. These numbers are called triangle numbers.

On the right you can see what happens if we subtract a triangle number from the triangle number after it. You can see from the pictures why this happens. You are taking away the left-hand part of the triangle in each case.

$3 - 1 = 2$
$6 - 3 = 3$
$10 - 6 = 4$
$15 - 10 = 5$
$21 - 15 = 6$

Counting numbers

On the right you can see what happens if we add one triangle number to the triangle number after it. The reason why this happens is explained on page 43. It is called a square number.

$1 + 3 = 4$
$3 + 6 = 9$
$6 + 10 = 16$
$10 + 15 = 25$
$15 + 21 = 36$

Square numbers

Remember... Triangle numbers build on themselves downward.

Word check
Triangle number: A number of objects that can be arranged into rows forming the pattern of a triangle.

Squares of numbers

We saw how patterns of numbers could be made from triangles on the previous page. More patterns can be made from square numbers.

Here are some strawberries arranged in squares.

Count the number of strawberries in each square. These numbers are called square numbers.

     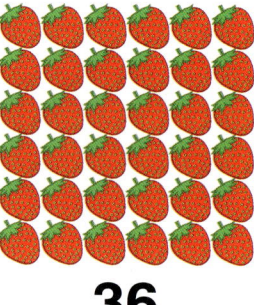

1   4   9   16   25   36

Square roots

Notice that square patterns are built up with the same number of shapes on each side. So:

$6 \times 6 = 36$

The number from which the square number **36** was made is **6**. This is known as the square root of **36**.

Look what happens if we subtract a square number from the square number after it.

4 − 1 = 3
9 − 4 = 5
16 − 9 = 7
25 − 16 = 9
36 − 25 = 11

Pattern of odd numbers

The answers are the sequence of odd numbers. You can see from the pictures why this happens.

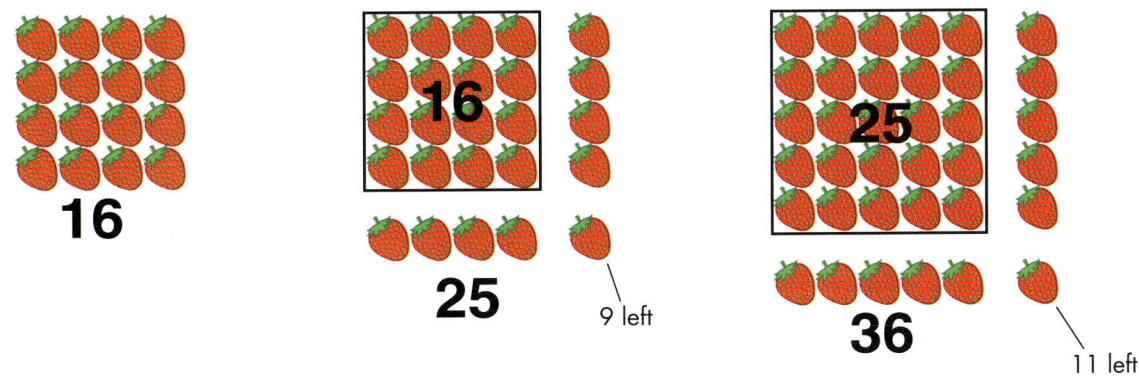

When you add one triangle number (page 40) to the next triangle number you get a square number.

Remember... Squares are made by multiplying together their square roots.

Word check

Square number: The number of a collection of objects that can be arranged in a square. It is the product of two equal numbers (for example, 16 is the square number produced by 4 × 4).

Square root: The number that, when multiplied by itself, produces a square number.

What symbols mean

Here is a list of the common math symbols together with an example of how they are used. You will find this list in each of the *Math Matters!* books, so that you can turn to any book if you want to look up the meaning of a symbol.

− Between two numbers this symbol means "subtract" or "minus." In front of one number it means the number is negative. In Latin *minus* means "less."

+ The symbol for adding. We say it "plus." In Latin *plus* means "more."

× The symbol for multiplying. We say it "multiplied by" or "times."

= The symbol for equals. We say it "equals" or "makes." It comes from a Latin word meaning "level" because weighing scales are level when the amounts on each side are equal.

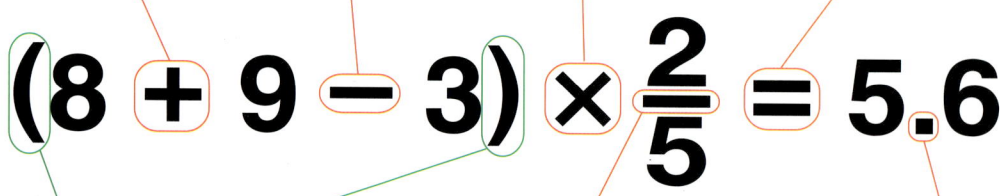

$(8 + 9 − 3) \times \dfrac{2}{5} = 5.6$

( ) Parentheses. You do everything inside the parentheses first. Parentheses always occur in pairs.

—, /, and ÷ Three symbols for dividing. We say it "divided by." A pair of numbers above and below a / or − make a fraction, so ⅖ or $\frac{2}{5}$ is the fraction two-fifths.

. This is a decimal point. It is a dot written after the units when a number contains parts of a unit as well as whole numbers. This is the decimal number five point six or five and six-tenths.

Glossary

Terms commonly used in this book.

Circle: A loop whose boundary is the same distance from the center all the way around..

Coordinates: The pair of numbers that tells you the position of a point on a graph. They are usually enclosed with parentheses.

Counting: Finding the total in a set of things by giving each item a number one more than the last one used.

Decimal point: A dot written after the units when a number contains parts of a unit as well as whole numbers.

Degree: A small part of a complete turn. There are 360 degrees in a complete turn.

Denominator: The number written on the bottom of a fraction.

Digit: The numerals 1, 2, 3, 4, 5, 6, 7, 8, 9, or 0. Several may be used to stand for a larger number. They are called digits to make it clear that they are only part of a complete number. So we might say, "The second digit is 4," meaning the second numeral from the left. Or we might say, "That is a two-digit number," meaning that it has two numerals in it, tens and units.

Equation: A number sentence using the = symbol, telling us that two different ways of writing a number are the same. For example, $2 + 2 = 4$ and $9 - 5 = 4$.

Flat: A large square representing 100. It can also be made up of ten "longs" put side by side.

Line graph: A graph on which a line is drawn through a set of points.

Long: A long shape representing 10.

Longitude: Angles that mark the distance of places east or west of Greenwich.

Minus numbers: The numbers that fall below zero on a number line (scale). Minus numbers or zero cannot be used for counting, only for measuring things like temperature. Minus numbers are also called negative numbers.

Multiple: A number of objects that can be rearranged into several rows of equal length and longer than just one.

Number: One or more numerals placed together represent the size of something (e.g., 45 is the numerals four and five placed together to represent the number forty-five).

Numeral: A symbol standing for a number. (The modern numerals are: 0, 1, 2, 3, 4, 5, 6, 7, 8, 9. Roman numerals are I, V, X, etc.)

Numerator: The number written on the top of a fraction.

Ordered numbers: Numbers used for putting things in order, such as first, second, third, fourth, fifth, and so on. Also called "ordinal numbers." *See* Unordered numbers.

Ordering: Putting numbers in order of size, for which the symbols < and > are very useful.

Place: The way we arrange numerals so that we know the value of a digit in a number.

Pole: The North and South Poles are the two points on the earth's surface around which the earth spins.

Powers: Little symbols written above the line, like the 4 in 10^4.

Prime number: A number that is not a multiple of anything (2, 3, 5, 7, 11, 13, 17, 19, etc., are prime numbers).

Rounding: Making a number shorter.

Scale: A set of marks on a line used for measuring.

Set: A collection of things we are interested in.

Significant figures: The numbers (reading from the left) that you need for your purpose. This is a way of describing how precise the number is. It is not affected by the position of the decimal point, which has more to do with the units being used.

Square number: The number of a collection of objects that can be arranged in a square. It is the product of two equal numbers (for example, 16 is the square number produced from 4×4).

Square root: The number that, multiplied by itself, produces a square number.

Symbol: A mark written on paper or something else to stand for a letter, a number, or an idea of any kind.

Time zone: A band of the earth sharing the same time. Time zones vary with longitude.

Triangle number: A number of objects that can be arranged into rows forming the pattern of a triangle.

Unit: 1 of something. A small, square shape representing 1.

Unordered numbers: Numbers used for counting when the order does not matter, such as one, two, three, four, five, and so on. Also called "cardinal numbers" or "counting numbers." *See* Ordered numbers.

Whole number: A number containing only complete units, not parts of units (it does not contain decimals or fractions).

Set index

USING THE SET INDEX

The 13 volumes in the *Math Matters!* set are:

Volume number	Title
1:	**Numbers**
2:	**Adding**
3:	**Subtracting**
4:	**Multiplying**
5:	**Dividing**
6:	**Decimals**
7:	**Fractions**
8:	**Shape**
9:	**Size**
10:	**Tables and Charts**
11:	**Grids and Graphs**
12:	**Chance and Average**
13:	**Mental Arithmetic**

An example entry:

Index entries are listed alphabetically.

numerator **6:** 32, 33; **7:** 7, 36

The volume number is shown in bold for each entry. In this case the index entry for "numerator" is found in two titles: **Decimals** and **Fractions**.

The page references in each volume are shown in regular type. In this case pages 32 and 33 of the tile **Decimals** and pages 7 and 36 of the title **Fractions**.

A

abacus **1:** 6
acute angle **8:** 9, 18
adding **2:** 4–5, 6–7, 8–9; **13:** 20–23, 34, 35, 36, 39
    decimals **2:** 36–37; **6:** 14–17
    fractions **2:** 40–41; **7:** 10–11, 16, 17, 22, 23, 27, 28, 29
    improper fractions **7:** 28
    large numbers **2:** 35
    minus numbers **2:** 38–39
    mixed fractions **7:** 16–17
    mixed numbers **7:** 29
    similar fractions **7:** 10–11
    single-digit numbers **2:** 6–25
    three-digit numbers **2:** 32–33
    two-digit numbers **2:** 28–29
    unlike fractions **7:** 22–23
    using columns **2:** 16–17
    using patterns **2:** 12–13
    using rulers **2:** 10–11
    using shapes **2:** 26–27
adding and subtracting **3:** 8
adding facts **2:** 14–15, 20–23; **3:** 16
adding on **13:** 26–27, 30–31
adding square **2:** 20–21, 24–25
angles **8:** 6–11, 44; **9:** 4, 34–41
    triangles **9:** 38, 39, 40, 41
apex **8:** 41
Arabic numerals **1:** 9
arc **8:** 38; **9:** 35
area **9:** 4, 18–29
    rectangles **9:** 20–21, 26, 27, 28, 29
    squares **9:** 18–19, 24–25
    triangles **9:** 22–23, 24, 25, 26, 27
arrowheads **8:** 31, 33
average **12:** 22–39
    mean **12:** 26–27, 29, 33
    median **12:** 24–25, 27, 28 34–35, 36–37
    mode **12:** 22–23, 27, 28, 34–37
axes **10:** 16, 18, 23; **11:** 16, 17

B

Babylonian number systems **1:** 12, 14
bar charts **10:** 16–17, 18, 21
base **9:** 22
big numbers **1:** 26–27
boundary **8:** 38; **9:** 6, 7

C

calculator check
    decimals **6:** 36
    factors, multiples, and products **4:** 13
    percentages **7:** 37, 41
    square roots **4:** 17
    Turn-Around Rule **4:** 11
capacity **9:** 5, 31
cards **12:** 10, 12, 13
carrying **2:** 23, 28, 29, 30, 31, 33, 35; **5:** 22, 23
categories **10:** 9, 16, 17, 18, 19
chance **12:** 6–21
    decimal numbers **12:** 14–15
    dice **12:** 5, 13, 16–17
    equal chance **12:** 10, 11, 13
    even **12:** 8–9
    fractions **12:** 14–15
    meaning of **12:** 6–7
    percentages **12:** 14–15
    ratios **12:** 14–15, 42–43
charts **10:** 5, 12, 13, 16–43
Chinese numerals **1:** 8
circles **8:** 38, 39
circles and triangles **9:** 35
circular protractor **10:** 43
circumference **8:** 38; **9:** 12, 13, 14, 15
clocks **1:** 13, 15
column charts **10:** 17, 18–19, 20, 21, 22, 23, 38
comparing decimals **6:** 42–43
computers **1:** 13
cones **8:** 40, 42, 43
conversion graphs **11:** 28–37
    Celsius to Fahrenheit **11:** 36–37
    centimeters to inches **11:** 32–33
    Fahrenheit to Celsius **11:** 36–37
    gallons to liters **11:** 28–29
    inches to centimeters **11:** 32–33
    kilograms to pounds **11:** 34–35
    kilometers to miles **11:** 30–31
    liters to gallons **11:** 28–29
    miles to kilometers **11:** 30–31
    pounds to kilograms **11:** 34–35
coordinates **1:** 37; **11:** 14, 16, 18, 19, 20
counting **1:** 7, 12, 22; **2:** 6–7; **3:** 6–7, 10–11
counting numbers **1:** 38

counting systems **1:** 12–13, 22–23
cubes **8:** 40, 41
cubic unit **9:** 31
cuboid **9:** 31
cuneiform writing **1:** 7
cylinders **8:** 40, 42, 43

D

data **10:** 5, 6–7, 9
data table **10:** 8–9
decimal currencies **6:** 10–11
decimal number **6:** 4, 6–7, 8–9
decimal place **6:** 22, 23, 25, 26, 27
decimal point **6:** 6–7, 8–9, 28, 29, 41
decimals **6:** 4, 5, 6–7, 8–9; **13:** 19
    dividing **5:** 26–27
decimal system **6:** 4, 10
degrees **1:** 12, 13, 14; **9:** 34
denominator **6:** 32–33; **7:** 7, 36
designs **8:** 40, 41, 42
diagonal **8:** 30, 31
diameter **8:** 38; **9:** 12, 13, 14, 16, 17
digit **1:** 16; **6:** 31
discount **7:** 41
disk **8:** 42, 43
distance charts **2:** 34–35
dividing **5:** 4–5, 6–7, 8–9, 10–11
    decimals **5:** 26–27; **6:** 30–31, 32, 33, 40–41
    fractions **5:** 30, 31, 34–35
dividing line **5:** 34–35; **7:** 7
division equations **5:** 42–43
division fact **5:** 16

E

easy pairs **13:** 12–13, 14, 15
Egyptian numerals **1:** 8
enlarging shapes **9:** 42–43
equals **1:** 24–25; **2:** 42–43
equations **2:** 42–43; **3:** 8, 9, 42–43; **4:** 8, 9, 30, 31, 42–43
equilateral triangle **7:** 9; **8:** 12, 13, 14, 18, 19, 21, 23, 41; **9:** 34
equivalent fractions **5:** 36–37; **7:** 16–21
even numbers **1:** 38; **3:** 14–15, 16, 17
exchanging method of subtracting **3:** 24–25, 30, 31, 32, 33, 35; **6:** 18–19; **13:** 28

F

fact family **3:** 17
factors **4:** 12–13
flats **1:** 18, 19; **6:** 8, 9
flip symmetry **8:** 22, 23, 24, 25, 26, 27
formula **9:** 10, 11

fractions **7:** 4–5, 6–7
    adding **7:** 10–11, 16, 17, 22, 23, 27, 28, 29
    bigger than one — *see* improper fractions
    comparing **7:** 19
    conversion from decimals **6:** 32–33
    conversion to decimals **6:** 38–39
    multiplying **7:** 12–13
    subtracting **7:** 24–25, 31
    writing **7:** 7
fractions and division **5:** 30, 31, 34–35

G

gate check **10:** 12, 13
gear ratio **7:** 33
geometry symbols **8:** 44
glossary **1–13:** 45
graph **11:** 4, 16–43
Greek numerals **1:** 9
grids **11:** 8, 9, 10, 11
grouping data **10:** 26, 27

H

halves **7:** 6
halving and adding **13:** 36, 39
halving and doubling **13:** 37
height **9:** 22, 30
hexagon **8:** 12, 13, 43
Hindu numerals **1:** 9

I

improper fractions **7:** 26–27, 28, 29, 30
inside angle **8:** 6, 15, 30
isosceles triangle **8:** 18, 19, 32; **9:** 41

K

kites **8:** 31, 33

L

latitude **11:** 8, 9
length **9:** 4, 6, 8, 12, 16–17, 18, 20, 22, 30
less than **1:** 24–25
line charts **10:** 38–39
line equations **11:** 24, 25, 26, 27
line graphs **1:** 36–37; **10:** 36–37; **11:** 23–43
line of symmetry **8:** 22
long division **5:** 18–19, 24–25, 27
longitude **1:** 14, 15; **11:** 8, 9
long multiplication **4:** 32–39, 41
longs **1:** 18, 19; **5:** 10–11; **6:** 8, 9

M

many-fold symmetry **8:** 24–25
maps **11:** 6–13
mental arithmetic **13:** 4–5, 6, 8
mental map **11:** 6–7
minus **3:** 8, 9, 37
minus coordinates **11:** 20
minus numbers **1:** 30–31; **3:** 37, 38, 39
mixed numbers **7:** 26, 27, 28–29
more than **1:** 24–25
multiples **1:** 35, 38; **4:** 12–13, 14
multiplication and division **5:** 16, 17
multiplication facts **4:** 18, 19, 22; **5:** 9, 16, 17
multiplication square **4:** 18–21, 22; **13:** 32, 33
multiplication tables **4:** 18, 19, 22–23; **13:** 32, 33
multiplying **4:** 4–5, 6; **13:** 20, 21, 32–33, 34, 35, 40, 41
    decimal numbers **4:** 40–41; **6:** 22–29
    fractions **7:** 12–13
    using grids **4:** 8, 9, 10, 11, 27, 32–33, 36–37
    using parentheses **4:** 30–31
    using pictures **4:** 7, 8, 9, 10, 11

N

near doubles **13:** 38–39
nets **8:** 40 — *see* designs
number line **2:** 10
number patterns **1:** 38–43
number squares **1:** 42–43
number triangles **1:** 40–41, 43
numbered categories **10:** 24, 25
numbers **1:** 4–5
    as decimals **1:** 32–33
    as fractions **1:** 32–33
    as graphs **1:** 36–37
    as shapes **1:** 18–19
    as symbols — *see* numerals
    origins **1:** 6–7
numerals **1:** 8–11, 17
numerator **6:** 32, 33; **7:** 7, 36

O

obtuse angle **8:** 9, 18
octagon **8:** 12, 13
odd numbers **1:** 38; **13:** 14, 15, 16, 17
odds **12:** 42–43
options **12:** 13
ordered numbers **1:** 22–23; **11:** 18
outside angle **8:** 6, 30
ovals **8:** 38, 39

P

parallelograms **8:** 15, 31, 34–35
parentheses **4:** 30–31
pentagon **8:** 12, 13, 43
per, a word for divide **5:** 38–39
percent **7:** 36–43; **13:** 36, 37
    conversion to fractions **7:** 38–39
percentage — see percent
percent less **7:** 42–43
percent more **7:** 40–41
perimeter **9:** 6–15
    circles **9:** 12–15
    pentagon **9:** 8
    rectangles **9:** 8, 10–11
    squares **9:** 10–11
perpendicular lines **8:** 9, 16, 17
pi **1:** 15; **6:** 39; **9:** 14, 15
pictograms **10:** 14, 15, 16
pie-chart measurer **10:** 41
pie charts **10:** 40–43
place value **1:** 2, 16–17, 18, 19; **2:** 2; **3:** 2; **4:** 2; **5:** 2; **6:** 2; **7:** 2; **9:** 2; **10:** 2; **13:** 2
plus numbers **3:** 38, 39
polyhedron **8:** 41
powers **1:** 27
prime factors **4:** 14, 15
prime numbers **1:** 34, 35, 38; **4:** 14–15
products **4:** 12–13
proportion **7:** 34–35
protractor **9:** 35
pyramids **8:** 41

Q

quadrilaterals **8:** 13, 30–31
quarters **7:** 6, 8–9, 10–11, 12

R

radius **8:** 18, 19, 38; **9:** 13
rainfall charts **10:** 34–35
range **12:** 30–33, 34, 36–37
ratios **5:** 40–41; **7:** 32–33, 35
ray **8:** 9
rectangles **8:** 25, 31, 36–37
recurring decimals **6:** 33, 34–35, 39
reflection **8:** 22, 23
regrouping **13:** 29
regrouping method of subtracting **3:** 26–27, 28, 29; **6:** 20–21
regular shapes **8:** 12–13
remainder **5:** 22, 23, 24, 25, 28–31, 39
    as a decimal **5:** 39
    as a fraction **5:** 30–31
rhombus **8:** 31, 35
right angle **8:** 8, 9, 18, 44; **9:** 34
right-angled triangles **8:** 16–17, 18, 21
rods **8:** 40, 42, 43
Roman numerals **1:** 10–11
rounding **1:** 28–29; **7:** 41
    decimals **6:** 28, 29, 36–37
    down **1:** 28–29
    up **1:** 28–29

S

samples **12:** 40–41
scale **10:** 20–21, 22, 23, 29, 34
scales **11:** 14, 16
sectors **8:** 39
set square **9:** 34, 38, 39
shape **8:** 4–5
sharing **5:** 8–9
short division **5:** 12–15, 22, 26
short multiplication **4:** 24-27
Sieve of Eratosthenes **4:** 15
significant figures **6:** 42, 43
similar fractions **7:** 10–11
size **9:** 4–5
solid shapes **8:** 40–43; **9:** 30–33
sorting category **10:** 16, 18
spheres **8:** 40, 43
splitting-up numbers **13:** 8–9
Splitting-Up Rule **4:** 30–31
spread **10:** 32, 33; **12:** 30–31, 33, 37, 38–39
square numbers **4:** 16–17, 20
square roots **1:** 42, 43; **4:** 16–17
squares **8:** 12, 13, 15, 24, 31, 37
straight angle **8:** 9, 10, 11; **9:** 38
subtracting **3:** 4–5; **13:** 24–31, 34, 35
    across zero **3:** 36–39
    decimals **3:** 32–33; **6:** 18–21
    fractions **3:** 40–41; **7:** 24–25, 31
    improper fractions **7:** 30
    large numbers **3:** 28–29
    minus numbers **3:** 37, 38, 39
    mixed numbers **7:** 30–31
    numbers with zeros **3:** 30–31
    similar fractions **3:** 40–41
    single-digit numbers **3:** 20–21, 22
    two-digit numbers **3:** 22–23
    using columns **3:** 20–23, 28–33
    using number lines **3:** 8–9, 12–13, 36–37
    using patterns **3:** 10, 14–17
    using rulers **3:** 8–9, 12–13
    using shapes **3:** 18–24
subtracting and dividing **5:** 6–7
subtracting facts **3:** 14–17
Sumerian numbers **1:** 7
symbols **1–13:** 44
symmetry **8:** 22–27

T

tables **10:** 5, 8–9, 10–11, 12–13
tally charts **10:** 12, 13, 14, 15, 16, 18
tallying **10:** 12–13
tessellating shapes **8:** 28–29
tetrahedron **8:** 41
three-dimensional (3D) shapes **8:** 4, 40, 41, 43
time charts **10:** 28–31
times tables **4:** 22–23
total **4:** 13
trapeziums **8:** 31, 32–33
triangles **8:** 14–19, 22–23, 28, 29, 32, 39
Turn-Around Rule **2:** 18–19, 25; **4:** 10-11, 18, 19, 22, 35; **13:** 10, 11
turning symmetry **8:** 23, 24–25, 26, 27
two-dimensional (2D) shapes **8:** 4, 12–39

U

unit **6:** 8, 9; **7:** 12
units **1:** 18, 19
    in division **5:** 10–11
unit squares **9:** 18–19
unordered numbers **1:** 22–23
using pictures **13:** 6–7

V

vertex **8:** 7, 41
volumes **9:** 4, 5, 30–33
    cuboid **9:** 30–31
    cylinder **9:** 32
    pyramid **9:** 33
    rod **9:** 32

W

whole number **1:** 17, 35
whole numbers **6:** 5, 6
width **9:** 11, 18, 20, 22, 30

X

x-axis **11:** 16, 20

Y

y-axis **11:** 16, 20

Z

zero **1:** 20–21, 26, 27